JACKIE WIBBLE WOBBLE & ME

by **Laurie Ahern**

illustrated by **Penny Weber**

ISBN: 978-1-63760-107-5

Laurie Ahern
14 Independence Way
Plum Island, Newbury, MA 01951
Ahern5478@gmail.com
JackieWibbleWobble.com

Juliet ♥ Belle ♥ Kiera ♥

1.2. 3.

This book is a gift to you
For all you have given to me
Love, Nannie

Jackie Wibble Wobble came home one day
She was a tiny, fuzzy yellow duck,
who always wanted to play

She liked to be held and cuddle with me
After all, she was a baby –
don't you see

But then you know,
she started to grow

Her feathers turned white
And her beak got longer and her eyes were
quite bright

She became my best friend
and I love her so much
I always feel safe when she's
nearby to touch

She follows me here and she follows me there

And together we can go
almost anywhere!

Jackie Wibble Wobble is loveable and so very sweet

And she loves to kiss me with her
cute yellow beak

She likes shiny buttons, if you have a few on,
you might start to laugh when you find them all gone

On my first day of school to the bus stop I went
And Jackie Wibble Wobble was quacking
behind me and then,

I got on the bus and she turned back around
And she wobbled her way to our house in the town

When I came home from school
at the end of the day

she was waiting for me – and guess what?
she wanted to play

I thought to myself, lots of
love to be had,
With Jackie Wibble Wobble
in my life
I am so very glad

She loves to be patted and loves to be hugged
And just like me,

We love to be loved

CPSIA information can be obtained
at www.ICGtesting.com
Printed in the USA
BVHW051455221121
622050BV00002B/23